Mind Control Supremacy

*Learn How to Change
People's Beliefs and
Behaviors by Unlocking and
Mastering the Mystery of
Human Psychology and
Persuasion*

Introduction

The earliest occurrence of the word *brainwashing* in the English language was October 7, 1950. It was written in an article by Edward Hunter, and published in an article in *Miami News*. The subject of his article was Chinese brainwashing. It spread like wildfire and was soon a popular phrase in news headlines that referred to the ongoing Cold War.

The term xi nao, meaning "wash brain" in Chinese suggests the meaning of this phrase. Xi nao is understood to describe the coercive persuasion methods that were used by the Maoist government. These techniques had the goal of transforming individuals from the imperialist side to "right-thinking" members of the Chinese social system.

There were several publications published following the Korean war that concluded brainwashing techniques were not being used by the Chinese government or in internment camps. Though the occurrence was disputed, the coined term *brainwashing* stuck around.

The ideology behind brainwashing later led the idea of mind control.

Only a decade later, in the 1960s, theories of mind control were used to describe the various workings of religious entities and the cult.The 1960s saw an upsurge in the number of Americans, particularly American youths that were quick to dedicate themselves to the various new religious movements.

These youths often suddenly adopted strange beliefs and behaviors before converting to the religion. In many cases, they even broke contact with family members and close friends. These strange and sudden behaviors left Americans wanting answers. The anti-cult movements delivered by implanting the idea of mind control.

Once the idea of mind control was suggest by anti-cult movements the media was quick to spread the idea to the masses; it spread like wildfire. Social scientists and psychologists worked to develop a sophisticated, organized model of mind control, one that would describe the change occurrences.

The population was split between people that believed this model could be accepted and those who thought there had to be a better explanation.

While it was mostly psychologists that were quick to jump onboard, social scientists did not believe the theories offered during this time adequately described the sudden religious conversion of America's youths.

Since the first idea of mind control decades ago there have been several other theories developed to describe the mind control ideology. Such a theory was developed by Kathleen Taylor, who believed that mind control was caused by the manipulation of the prefrontal cortex.

This made the individual more susceptible to black and white thinking, more likely to be influenced, thus, more susceptible to mind control. Robert Cialdini, on the other hand, believed that those using mind control were exploiting the unconscious rules of the human mind.

These rules govern human interactions and made individuals more likely to be persuaded to a specific way of acting or thinking.A third popular idea was developed by theorist Philip Zimbardo, who believed that mind control was the process that made individual freedom and choice almost impossible, because they were corrupted using modification or a distorted way of thinking.

The distorted or modified thinking would lead the individual to experience new cognitive, behavioral, motivational, and affect. All of these various theories led to the version of mind control that is accepted today.

In this book, we will discuss both the meaning and the nature of mind control. We will discuss how it can be used in conjunction with the areas of psychology and persuasion. Finally, we will discuss it's difference from brainwashing, mind control techniques, and how mind control can be used in your daily lives.

From this point onward, the term "subject" should be understood to mean the individual upon whom mind control is being exercised, i.e., the person being controlled. The term "controller" should be understood to mean the person that is performing the mind control, whether it be a therapist, family member, religious leader, or other controlling entity.

What is Mind Control?

After decades of theories and research, psychologists have only begun to agree on what the definition for mind control might be. Mind control is a process that often goes by many names, including thought reform, thought control, and coercive persuasion.

By definition, it is described as a theoretical indoctrination process through which influence over the mind is achieved. The process of mind control can impair an individual's ability to think independently, outside of what they are being told.

This often affects their affiliation, their behaviors, and their core beliefs. It is crucial to remember that real mind control is not about corrupting the brain. Rather, real mind control is about using persuasive techniques and psychological knowledge to change an individual's actions, thoughts, behaviors and/or core beliefs.

Mind control and brainwashing are two words that are often used interchangeably. While similar ideas have been used to explain the ideologies behind both of these terms, it is still important to remember that they are still very different processes.

They should not be used interchangeably, because they are understood to mean different things. Mind control is everywhere. It is not a technique that is only employed by government agencies and cults as some think.

There are several different ways which forms of mild control, mild and severe are present even in your daily lives. Milder forms of mind control are even seen in television commercials. How many times have you been staring at the television, in almost a trance state as a set of commercials interrupts your favorite show?

A commercial will come on that associate a fluffy teddy bear with dryer sheets or a popular chip brand with babies. While the baby and the teddy bear seem to have nothing to do with the product, your attention is drawn in by the unrelated positive imagery. This is a form of coercion, and also of mind control.

While it is not so severe as to make you want to change your mind about politics or your position on gun control, it is enough to make you consider buying the product, whether subconscious or not.

Even these subtle messages are considered a form of mind control. It is everywhere. Reading this book will help you recognize forms of mind control, notice its benefits, and even use it in your daily lives if you choose.

Benefits of Mind Control

What is the first thought that comes to your mind when you hear the term mind control? If you are like many individuals, you thought of a destructive process, one that manipulates the subject in a way that is undesirable to them.

It is often thought of as a tool used by cults and government agencies to gain followers and support. However, this negative stigma that surrounds mind control is not always the case.

If this is your idea of mind control, take a second and remember that mind control is not the same process of brainwashing. There are several positive techniques that can be used for mind control.

It also has the potential of benign beneficial on either end of the relationship, whether you are the subject or the controller. In this chapter we will discuss how mind control can be beneficial to the people involved on either end of the spectrum.

Benefits to the Subject

There are various types of mind control that can benefit the subject. Techniques such as hypnosis, self-hypnosis, brainwave entrainment and others that benefit the subject in a variety of ways. The benefits may include the correction of erroneous behaviors, alleviation of symptoms caused by various psychiatric disorders and improved reactions and attitudes.

One of the most beneficial uses of mind control is cessation of negative behaviors. Individuals, who smoke cigarettes, drink excessively, use illicit drugs, engage in dangerous sex or regularly engage in other risky or undesirable behaviors may benefit from mind control, as it can help them stop their behavior.

This is often done using hypnosis under the guidance of a therapist or can even be completed using some self-hypnosis or brainwave entrainment. A second benefit to mind control is its usefulness in treating various psychiatric difficulties.

Mind control has the potential to help individuals who suffer because of past events, depression, anxiety and other psychological problems. The techniques used for mind control in these cases are often taught by a therapist or psychologist.

They will help train the mind using hypnosis or some form of self-help, both of which may benefit the individual. This can make them forget past events, have a happier existence or even live a calmer lifestyle.The final benefit of mind control is the ability to change undesirable reactions or attitudes.

For example, some individuals are jealous to the point of insanity. They do not trust, are over cautious and destroy relationships because of these reasons. Rather than treating all scenarios as a reason to distrust, the mind can be trained to stop reacting in this way. Attitudes can also be changed.

A person who finds they are pessimistic and negative in many areas of life may benefit from mind control by being trained to be more positive.

Benefits to the Controller

When mind control is used for manipulative or persuasive purposes, it is likely that mind control will benefit the person that is in control, rather than the subject.An individual who is capable of using mind control may have an easier time persuading people to do activities they want, use their ideas, influencing people to listen to them and more.

While all forms of mind control are not necessarily bad, forms that benefit the controller rather than the subject can be considered destructive. The exception to this rule is types of mind control that would benefit both the subject and the controller.

How Mind Control Works

It is critical to remember that mind control is beneficial depending on its intended use. It is possible for mind control to be either destructive or constructive. It does have key benefits, but sometimes the benefits are experienced by the controller, and other times they are experienced by the subject.

In this chapter we will discuss how mind control works from both a destructive and a constructive viewpoint.

Destructive Mind Control

When considering the way that mind control works, it is important to remember that the perpetrator is somebody that the subject knows, and quite possibly, trusts. Individuals who practice the art of mind control on others must be close to the subject of mind control in order to work.

It is important to remember that as humans, we often summarize an individual's personality within the first few seconds of meeting them for the first time. Someone who is practiced the art of mind control assesses how useful the relationship may be to them upon meeting someone.

They do this by reading the subject's face, words, and body language to get a reading on their personality. Once the controller has a reading on the subject's personality, they will project their own persona. The goal of this is to create a close, intimate bond.

This bond allows the subject to open up to the controller, allowing them to assess strengths and weaknesses, uncover insecurities, and understand the things, both physical and not, that the subject values.

Then, the controller will use actions and words to get four important messages across. They will first convey that they like the person you are. Next, the controller coveys that they are very similar to the subject.

This creates trust, and allows for the third message; that the subject's secrets should be shared in confidence. Finally, the controller will aim to convince the subject that they are the perfect companion, friend, lover, etc., for the subject.

Controller's send these messages for several reasons. The first message is key because when the subject is liked they are more likely to feel noticed and accepted. This is a first step in getting someone to like you is making them feel that they accept you.

The second message, that the psychopath like the subject is also key. This strengthens the bond between controller and subject, making the subject more likely to trust. The controller will often share seemingly intimate details, only to strengthen the ties of their bond with the subject. However, these details are frequently lies.

Once the subject trusts the controller, they are more likely to share details about themselves, which can then be further used in the mind control process.

The fourth and final step is to project the idea that the controller and subject have the ideal bond between them. This bond is what allows them to so easily control the subject.This brings up a question...how does someone meeting new people and forming bonds in real life know that they are being manipulated?

Often, they do not. While bonds such as those built between husband and wife are very similar to this, they do have key differences. The relationship built between a controller and a subject is not real. It is built upon lies. Additionally, leaders will often stop trying to build the relationship once they are in the subject's head.

Once the subject is open to manipulation, they may begin doing the bare minimum to maintain the relationship and will not be loving. They may also discard the relationship once they find that having mind control over the subject is no longer beneficial to them.

Techniques for Deconstructive Mind Control

Once the subject has a strong bond built with the subject of their mind control they can use one of several techniques, often a combination, to exercise control. If the nature of the relationship is truly destructive, they may use some of the techniques listed in the BITE model of mind control, which allow for control of behavior, information, thoughts and/or emotion.

This can include controlling financials, sleep, access to information, manipulating thinking, or encouraging certain emotions that may or may not be damaging to the subject. The techniques used for mind control will be further discussed in Mind Control Techniques chapter.

Constructive Mind Control

It is important to remember that not all mind control is destructive. Mind control can benefit the subject, by allowing them to cease negative behaviors, have a better self-confidence, promote a positive attitude and more. When used for a positive purpose rather than a destructive purpose, the process used for mind control is quite different.

Constructive mind control seeks to change behaviors in a positive way. You may work with a guiding professional, such as a counselor or psychologists, or may be performing mind control on yourself.The first step of constructive mind control is often to allow the mind to enter a subconscious state.

The relaxed state that the mind must be in for constructive mind control too be effective is known as the alpha brain state. During this state, the right hemisphere of the brain is more active over the left.

This occurs several times throughout the day, including early in the morning when you are just beginning to wake up. Once the mind is in a relaxed state, the chosen mind control technique can be effective.

This works best with the Silva model, neuro-linguistic programming, hypnosis and self-hypnosis. The purpose of the state of the mind is to allow it to be trained.

While thought-stopping, rewards and punishments and other conscious techniques may still be able to benefit the subject, these often take longer to learn than the processes used when the mind is in its relaxed, vulnerable, learning state.

Mind Control vs. BrainWashing

Mind control and brainwashing are terms that are sometimes used interchangeably and often confused. Mind control and brainwashing are not the same process. While both are interwoven throughout history and derived from similar terminology, they are two very different terms.

The key differences between mind control and brainwashing include their understood meaning, the way they have been developed across history, the individual who is excising control and the techniques that are used.The understood meaning of mind controls vs brainwashing are very different.

Brainwashing is understood to be a process that causes individuals to radically change their beliefs, principles and/or actions. Does this sound like mind control? It isn't.The second part to the definition qualifies true brainwashing as being a sudden change that is caused by systematic or even forceful pressures, whether physical, mental, or both.

In contrast, mind control has a similar definition with using different processes. Mind control is also a process that aims to change beliefs, principles and/or actions. However, mind control is often excised using techniques aimed at psychological knowledge and persuasion to convince or manipulate someone into change.

While the results of mind control and brainwashing seem to be very similar, it is the techniques and methods used to achieve the changes that make up the core differences. Brainwashing and mind control also differ because of their appearances in history. The ideas were developed nearly a decade apart. The ideology behind brainwashing goes back to the 1950s.

At the time, it was believed that the Maoist government was using brainwashing in POW camps to transform individuals from imperialist beliefs to "right thinking" members of the Chinese social system. While it was later stated that these brainwashing techniques did not occur, the term was still coined. Though it still interested some, the fascination was lessened once the development of the ideas behind mind control appeared in the 1960s.

At the beginning of the 1960s mind control was used to describe the conversions toward the religious movement. Movements, the media and the masses began to notice an upsurge in the number of Americans, particularly younger ones, that suddenly adopted new religious beliefs.

These beliefs changed their thinking, their actions, and even the way they interacted with friends and family members. However, it was believed that the church was using techniques very different from the ones that the Chinese government was accused of using.

It was believed the Chinese government was using coercive, forceful techniques to brainwash, whereas the church was using persuasion of the subconscious and similar techniques to excise mind control. The members of the church were also at a different position in the lives of the American youth. They were often seen as friends, rather than enemies. This made them much easier to manipulate, thus, causing conversion.

The controller that excises mind control to affect a person's beliefs, thinking, or actions is also a key difference between brainwashing and mind control. Brainwashing is usually performed by an outside force. The outside force, or controller, in brainwashing is usually considered to be an enemy, or opponent. This includes figures such as government leaders or guards in a prison camp.

When mind control is excised by someone, the controller will be someone the victims knows, or even trusts. This can include parents, a teacher, a therapist, a friend, or even someone the subject has a close intimate relationship with.

The fourth and final difference between brainwashing is the techniques that are used. This is a critical difference. Mind control uses techniques that are often significantly less aggressive than the techniques of brainwashing. Brainwashing techniques are not necessarily always violent or aggressive, however, they are nearly always forceful to at least some extent. Mind control techniques are not as simply explained.

The techniques in mind control are often persuasive or manipulative exercise the control over someone else's thoughts, actions, and/or behaviors.

Mind Control Techniques

As we discuss mind control techniques, remember that not all mind control is destructive. In this chapter we will discuss techniques for mind control.

The information will cover both destructive and constructive techniques. The techniques discussed will include the BITE model, the Silva model, neuro-linguistic programming (NLP), hypnosis, self-hypnosis and brainwave entrainment.

The BITE Model (Destructive)

The BITE model is considered to be the most conclusive model of destructive mind control. It was developed by Steve Hassan. The name of this model is an acronym for behavior, information, thought and emotion. These four types of control are fully discussed, along with methods and techniques that can be used. As you read this list remember that not all of these techniques are entirely negative.

While this model is destructive as a whole, it does contain some positive techniques that may even be used for mind control. These include techniques such as thought-stopping and establishing a system of rewards and punishments to excise control. Though this model uses terminology that would apply to group control such as that used in colts, remember that it can be applied to the mind control of single people as well.

Steve Hassan's BITE Model

- Regulate individual's physical reality

- Dictate where, how, and with whom the member lives and associates or isolates

- When, how and with whom the member has sex

- Control types of clothing and hairstyles

- Regulate diet - food and drink, hunger and/or fasting

- Manipulation and deprivation of sleep

- Financial exploitation, manipulation or dependence

- Restrict leisure, entertainment, vacation time

- Major time spent with group indoctrination and rituals and/or self-indoctrination including the Internet

- Permission required for major decisions

- Thoughts, feelings, and activities (of self and others) reported to superiors

- Rewards and punishments used to modify behaviors, both positive and negative

- Discourage individualism, encourage group-think

- Impose rigid rules and regulations

- Instill dependency and obedience

Information Control

1. **Deception**:
   - Deliberately withhold information
   - Distort information to make it more acceptable
   - Systematically lie to the cult member

2. **Minimize or discourage access to non-cult sources of information, including:**
   - Internet, TV, radio, books, articles, newspapers, magazines, other media
   - Critical information
   - Former members
   - Keep members busy so they don't have time to think and investigate
   - Control through cell phone with texting, calls, internet tracking

3. Compartmentalize information into Outsider vs. Insider doctrines

- Ensure that information is not freely accessible

- Control information at different levels and missions within group

- Allow only leadership to decide who needs to know what and when

4. Encourage spying on other members

- Impose a buddy system to monitor and control member

- Report deviant thoughts, feelings and actions to leadership

- Ensure that individual behavior is monitored by group

5. Extensive use of cult-generated information and propaganda, including:

- Newsletters, magazines, journals, audiotapes, videotapes, YouTube, movies and other media

- Misquoting statements or using them out of context from non-cult sources

6. Unethical use of confession

- Information about sins used to disrupt and/or dissolve identity boundaries

- Withholding forgiveness or absolution

- Manipulation of memory, possible false memories

Thought Control

1. Require members to internalize the group's doctrine as truth

   - Adopting the group's 'map of reality' as reality

   - Instill black and white thinking

   - Decide between good vs. evil

   - Organize people into us vs. them (insiders vs. outsiders

2. Change person's name and identity

3. Use of loaded language and clichés which constrict knowledge, stop critical thoughts and reduce complexities into platitudinous buzz words

4. Encourage only 'good and proper' thoughts

5. Hypnotic techniques are used to alter mental states, undermine critical thinking and even to age regress the member

6. Memories are manipulated and false memories are created

7. Teaching thought-stopping techniques which shut down reality testing by stopping negative thoughts and allowing only positive thoughts, including:

- Denial, rationalization, justification, wishful thinking

- Chanting

- Meditating

- Praying

- Speaking in tongues

- Singing or humming

8. Rejection of rational analysis, critical thinking, constructive criticism

9. Forbid critical questions about leader, doctrine, or policy allowed

10. Labeling alternative belief systems as illegitimate, evil, or not useful

Emotional Control

1. Manipulate and narrow the range of feelings – some emotions and/or needs are deemed as evil, wrong or selfish

2. Teach emotion-stopping techniques to block feelings of homesickness, anger, doubt

3. Make the person feel that problems are always their own fault, never the leader's or the group's fault

4. Promote feelings of guilt or unworthiness, such as

   - Identity guilt

   - You are not living up to your potential

   - Your family is deficient

   - Your past is suspect

   - Your affiliations are unwise

   - Your thoughts, feelings, actions are irrelevant or selfish

   - Social guilt

- Historical guilt

5. Instill fear, such as fear of:

    - Thinking independently

    - The outside world

    - Enemies

    - Losing one's salvation

    - Leaving or being shunned by the group

    - Other's disapproval

6. Extremes of emotional highs and lows – love bombing and praise one moment and then declaring you are horrible sinner

7. Ritualistic and sometimes public confession of sins

8. Phobia indoctrination: inculcating irrational fears about leaving the group or questioning the leader's authority

    - No happiness or fulfillment possible outside of the group

- Terrible consequences if you leave: hell, demon possession, incurable diseases, accidents, suicide, insanity, 10,000 reincarnations, etc.

- Shunning of those who leave; fear of being rejected by friends, peers, and family

- Never a legitimate reason to leave; those who leave are weak, undisciplined, unspiritual, worldly, brainwashed by family or counselor, or seduced by money, sex, or rock and roll

- Threats of harm to ex-member and family

The Silva Model

The Silva model used in mind control can be used in correlation with other techniques. This model was developed Jose Silva. It combines the mind control techniques associated with neuro-linguistic programming, self-hypnosis, and meditation.

The goal is to train the brain to allow the subject to enter an alpha state and then use visualization to adopt new thoughts, attitudes and/or behaviors. The training of the mind to enter the alpha state consumes a large portion of the process for the Silva model. The mind is trained over a period of 50 consecutive days.

It is considered to be one of the most effective training exercises that will eventually allow your mind to enter the alpha state almost instantly. Each step of the program should be completed in the morning as soon as you are awake. It should not take more than 15 minutes. Each step in the training process should be completed for a period of ten days. For the first ten days, count backwards from 100 to 1.

Do this at a pace of 2 seconds between each number. For the next ten days, count backwards from 50 to 1 using the same pace as the previous exercises. For days 20-30, count backward from 25 to 1.

The following ten days, count backwards from 10 to 1. For the final ten days of the exercise, count backwards from 5 to 1. Be sure to keep the 2 seconds pace for counting through the duration of your programming.You may be thinking, it's that easy? All I have to do is count? Well, yes and no. While you are counting close your eyelids. Look slightly upwards, as this position is known to produce alpha brainwaves.

Once you have taught the brain to enter the alpha state, you may begin the process of visualization. If you are not familiar with visualization, you will also need techniques for this exercise. Begin with something easy, such as a piece of fruit that you can visualize in great detail. Picture it in front of you on a cinema-like screen, which is often referred to as the mental monitor.

As you picture the object of your choosing, try to resist thinking irrelevant thoughts. Allow your mind to focus solely on the object. Freeing your mind from distractive thoughts is key for the Silva model to work. If you do find that your mind begins to wander, bring it back to the object. Do not become frustrated if you become easily distracted in the beginning.

You will notice that as days go by, you will eventually think of less and less irrelevant thoughts until you have perfected your meditation process. The reason the Silva technique works is the amount of time that is spent in the alpha state. This passive form of mind control can open up the mind, improve extrasensory perception, and improve memory and overall health.

Neuro-Linguistic Programming

Neuro-linguistic programming is a form of mind control that uses language to train the brain. Before the linguistic programming begins, the mind should be in a relaxed, subconscious state.

It is often most effective when used throughout the night. As you slumber, recorded messages are played. These messages will often help you become more motivated, succeed at cessation of a bad habit, or have a more positive attitude.

Hypnosis

Hypnosis is a form of mind control that is considered to be very effective. It is highly used in the field of psychology, to stop negative behaviors, help with psychiatric disorders, and change the subject's outlook.

In order for hypnosis to work, the mind must be in a receptive, vulnerable, subconscious state. This allows messages to be imprinted in the brain, to teach it to either stop or start a certain behavior.

Hypnosis is most often performed under the guidance of a hypnotist or other psychologist trained in the field. It is most effective when performed with a psychologist that you trust, as it will be easier for your mind to enter a relaxed state around someone you know.

The hypnotist will entrance you into a deeply relaxed state, using repetitive movements, soothing vocals, or even music. Once you have entered this state, the hypnotist will say selected phrases that will be deeply etched into the brain for learning purposes.

Self-Hypnosis

If you are not comfortable having someone else perform hypnosis mind control on you, self-hypnosis can be used. When using self-hypnosis, it is important that the mind is in either the theta wave or alpha wave state. This is when the mind is operating at brain wave frequencies between 4 and 13Hz. There are several different things self-hypnosis is used for.

These include enhancing creativity, cessation of bad habits, improving sports performance, stopping pain, improving sexual health, increasing spirituality, encouraging mind development, improving overall health, and boosting self-confidence. If you find that you struggle with achieving an alpha or theta wave state yourself, you can use the techniques discussed in the section on the Silva model.

The 50 day training program will help you enter an alpha state almost instantly. However, the majority of recordings used for self-recording will instruct you on reaching an acceptable state of mind before working to alter your subconscious. Once you are an alpha or theta wave state, you will listen to a recording. There are many types of recordings available, depending on your specific goal when attempting self-hypnosis.

They may be able to boost your spiritual feelings, increase your self-confidence, stop your bad habits and more. Simply continue performing self-hypnosis on a regular basis, until you feel that your mind has been completely trained in the way you desire.

Brainwave Entrainment

Brainwave entrainment is the final mind control technique that we will discuss. As its name suggests, brainwave entrainment is a way to train your brain to promote a specific frequency of brainwaves. Brainwaves are the electrical pulses that are transmitted by the brain. They are measured using frequency, which is a measurement of the number of pulses that a neuron emits in a second.

However, it is important to remember that the human brain does not operate on a single frequency. The frequency measured will be determined by the frequency that has the most brainwaves. The underlying principle behind brainwave entrainment is the way that the human brain will react to external stimuli perceived using one of the five senses.

It often synchronizes the dominant brainwave of the brain with the external stimuli. Brainwave entrainment uses stimuli such as pulsing beats or light to train the brainwave to alter its frequency on demand. There are five ranges of brainwave frequency; Delta, Theta, Alpha,

Beta, and Gamma. They have frequencies from 00.9-4Hz, 4-7Hz, 7-13Hz, 13-30Hz, and 30-100Hz, respectively.

Brainwave entrainment uses four different types of stimuli to alter brain frequency; binaural beats, monaural beats, isochronic tones, and photic drive. Binaural beats are used to expand the limitation of the human ear, which is capable of registering frequencies between 20Hz and 20KHz. For binaural beats to be effective, you must wear headphones. You will be presented with two stable tones with slightly different frequencies.

This expands the limitations of the human ear. Monaural beats have the same goal, although they are played over a speaker. There are two tones played from separate speakers to create the effect. It is believed that monaural beats are more effective than binaural beats. Isochronic tones raise alter brainwaves using audio. It is a single tone that repeats at a set frequency. Photic drive techniques use pulsing light to entrain the brain. It is most frequently used in conjunction with audio tones.

Using Mind Control in Your Daily Lives

When used properly, the ability to control the minds of others can be very useful. You don't have to be a bad person or a deviant to practice mind control on others.

In this chapter we will discuss how to control a conversation and what techniques will be effective when trying to persuade people to your opinion or to do what you want.

Controlling the Conversation

There are three elements that can be used to exercise mind control in any conversation that you have in your daily lives. These include eye contact, voice project and verbal leading. The reason these three things are important is because they develop the controller to be the alpha in the relationship. The alpha role is associated with power, making it much simpler to control someone else's mind.

The role between alpha and beta is one that is present in any situation. Pay close attention next time you are going through the checkout line at the grocery store. Even this simple interaction will have an alpha and a beta role. One way to assert your role as an alpha is to maintain eye contact.

Looking someone in the eyes commands their attention. As you try to persuade someone of something, do not be afraid to come across as dominant. The more eye contact you make, the more dominant you will appear.

The more dominant you are in a conversation, the more likely it is that your mind control techniques will be successful. Voice projection is another key component of using mind control in your daily lives.

Voice projection is the clarity and volume of someone's voice. Pay attention while you observe the conversations of others. The alpha is the person with the louder, clearer voice. Therefore, people who can project their voices are considered to have higher value in social situations.

They are the ones that are most likely to be successful at mind control techniques. When you project your voice, you seem more interesting to some people. This makes them feel more comfortable around, making them more susceptible to persuasion.

Once you have begun to use eye contact and vocal projection when you interact with others in social situations, you will begin to develop the alpha mindset. The alpha mindset is what will give you the power to control others.

The next step is verbal leading. As you interact in social conversations, it is important that the alpha leads. This means the alpha sets the tone, topic, and flow of the conversation. Once you are able to verbally lead, make eye contact, and project vocally, you will be able to lead any conversation, allowing you to use further mind control.

Techniques Once You're in Control

Once you have someone's attention and are controlling the conversation, you can say whatever you would like. This is the time that it is essential to implement mind control techniques.

Some of the techniques you can use for mind control in your daily lives include thinking for someone, leaving bread crumbs, using emotions to convince people and repeating your point until it is clear.

Do the Thinking for Them

How often has someone told you to think something over? And how many times have you been distracted by other things in your life and never given the idea a thought again? When trying to convince someone to do what you want, layout a presentation of why they should listen to you.

For example, if you are trying to convince your spouse to start a 401K you should lay out all of the information in front of them. Have all the benefits, the monthly costs, total amounts, how it will fit into your budget and any other relevant information (employer benefits) that may help persuade them to your idea.

 Do not just give them the idea and tell them to critically consider it, do the thinking for them.

Leaving Bread Crumbs

Have you ever heard the expression "give them an inch and they will take a mile?" Oftentimes, if you can convince someone to listen to a part of your opinion you will have them hooked.

Once they are hooked you will be free to give them the rest of the information they need. The best way to do this is to drop interesting tidbits of information that pertain to the point you are trying to make. Once you have gained their attention on a related topic, mind control will be so much simpler.

Using Emotions

Do you ever notice how commercials use emotions to sell their product or raise donations? Abused animals and starving children are used to collect monthly donations.

Puppies and babies that generate a warm, fuzzy feeling are used to sell lotions, tires, or even bath tissue. The reason emotions are so effective in selling products is because they allow access to the mind.

Once access is granted any types of subliminal messages and mind control can be exercised over the brain. You can also use this technique in your daily lives. When you are trying to convince someone of your opinion, play on their emotions.

If you are trying to convince a friend to come to lunch at a new spot, say something along the lines of "you have no idea how much it would mean to me." This will often be effective.

Repetition

Do you have a friend or relative that is obsessed with their political viewpoint, food health, or another annoying topic? Have you ever broke down and listened to what they had to say, just because they have repeated the same thing so much?

While you should not aim to irritate people to an extreme, you should try to repeat yourself often enough that your ideology begins to sink in. Once you have penetrated someone's mind to even the smallest extent exercising control of their mind will be a much more likely possibility.

Frequently Asked Questions

Does mind control really work?

Yes, mind control really does work. Over the course of time, neurological science and psychology has proven the ways that mind control work. The mind really is susceptible to alteration during certain brainwave states.

Additionally, it is proven that alphas are more likely to be listened to and that several mind control techniques can be used for persuasion in your daily lives.

Will I be able to tell if I am under mind control?

It can be very difficult for someone to know if they are being affected by mind control. However, if you critically evaluate your relationship with someone you may be able to uncover manipulative or controlling relationships that are subject to mind control. If you find that someone frequently lies to you about their past or makes up things to make you relate to them, you may be a subject of mind control. Controllers often try to relate to their subjects and gain trust before exercising mind control.

Additionally, you may be able to tell if mind control is being used if the nature of your relationship with someone drastically shifts. Once a controller earns your trust and confidence they will often stop trying to maintain the relationship. A third indicator is sudden behavioral changes by you, or estrangement from your family and friends. However, if you are under mind control you will often try to rationalize these sudden changes. Though there are some red flags, it is very difficult to tell if you are under mind control.

Can anyone perform mind control?

Yes, anyone can perform mind control. However, you will only be able to perform mind control if you are capable of accepting an alpha role. You can begin to establish your alpha role by using eye contract, voice projection, and vocal leading.

When you do these activities, you will be better able to accept the alpha role. Fitting into the alpha role will allow you to lead conversations and use mind control techniques to get the things that you want.

How do I know if my friend/lover/etc. is using mind control on me?

The easiest way to tell if your lover, friend, or someone else is using mind control on you is to critically examine your behaviors and your relationship. If you have had sudden behavior changes, ask yourself why? If you try to rationalize but do not have a valid reason, it is likely that you are the subject of mind control. You can also tell by examining the nature of your relationship.

If the other person is using control over you, whether financially, using food, or another method, they may be using mind control too. You can also tell if your relationship seems to have a drastic change after a certain period of time. If the other person in your relationship stops trying once they have gained your trust, they may be using you as a subject for mind control.

Isn't mind control for cults, or government agencies?

The original ideologies behind mind control were believed to only be used by cults and government agencies. However, mind control can really be used by anybody. It can be used by our boss, our friends, our lovers, our teachers, members of our church, literally anyone who might be able to excise control over the relationship.

Is mind control always bad?

No, mind control is not always bad. There are many types of mind control that can be destructive in nature, which cause the subject to think or act in ways that they normally would not. However, there are other types of mind control that are used to benefit the subject.

This includes self-hypnosis, hypnosis, the Silva model, brainwave entrainment and other methods that will help the subject in different areas. This can include health, cessation of bad habits, stress relief and more.

Conclusion

The development of the ideas and techniques behind mind control have taken decades to develop. During this time, several stigmas were also developed, many of which are not true. The ideology behind brainwashing was developed only a decade before mind control. Though they stem from similar ideas, they are not the same and cannot be used interchangeably.

Mind control was also once believed to only be used by government organizations and cults. This is another stigma that is not true. Mind control can be used by anyone, anywhere, at any time. It is also important to remember that mind control is not always bad. There are several key advantages to using and being under mind control. When you make the decision to use mind control on those you encounter, you are making the decision to take control of your own life.

When you decide to undergo mind control processes yourself, you may find several health benefits, as well as the cessation of bad habits. Your benefits will depend on your specific goal with mind control. While mind control and brainwashing stemmed from similar ideas, only decades apart, it is crucial to remember that they are not the same. Mind control is completed by people we know.

As a result, you can use mind control in your daily lives to get the things that you want. You can do this by being the alpha in any conversation and using coercive techniques to convince others of your ideas.

www.ingramcontent.com/pod-product-compliance
Lightning Source LLC
Chambersburg PA
CBHW071116280526
45787CB00003B/1074